The American Poetry Series

Vol. 1, Sandra McPherson, *Radiation*

Vol. 2, David Young, *Boxcars*

Vol. 3, Al Lee, *Time*

Vol. 4, James Reiss, *The Breathers*

Vol. 5, Louise Glück, *The House on Marshland*

Vol. 6, David McElroy, *Making It Simple*

Vol. 7, Dennis Schmitz, *Goodwill, Inc.*

Vol. 8, John Ashbery, *The Double Dream of Spring*

Vol. 9, Lawrence Raab, *The Collector of Cold Weather*

Vol. 10, Stanley Plumly, *Out-of-the-Body Travel*

Vol. 11, Louise Bogan, *The Blue Estuaries*

Vol. 12, John Ashbery, *Rivers and Mountains*

Vol. 13, Laura Jensen, *Bad Boats*

Vol. 14, John Ashbery, *Some Trees*

Vol. 15, Sandra McPherson, *The Year of Our Birth*

Vol. 16, John Crowe Ransom, *Selected Poems*

Vol. 17, Robert Hass, *Praise*

Vol. 18, James Tate, *Riven Doggeries*

Vol. 19, Dennis Schmitz, *String*

Vol. 20, Louise Glück, *Descending Figure*

Vol. 21, John Logan, *Only the Dreamer Can Change the Dream*

Vol. 22, James Tate, *The Lost Pilot*

Vol. 23, Sandra McPherson, *Elegies for the Hot Season*

Vol. 24, Sandra McPherson, *Patron Happiness*

Vol. 25, Jon Anderson, *The Milky Way*

Vol. 26, Louise Glück, *Firstborn*

Vol. 27, Stanley Plumly, *Summer Celestial*

Books by Stanley Plumly

Giraffe
How the Plains Indians Got Horses
In the Outer Dark
Out-of-the-Body Travel
Summer Celestial

35
0
signed
98

Summer Celestial

for Robin —

from James Parse

Stanley Plumly

Apr 9. 86
NYC

Summer Celestial

Stanley Plumly

THE ECCO PRESS

NEW YORK

❧ ❧

It is a flaw

In happiness to see beyond our bourn—

It forces us in Summer skies to mourn

KEATS

First published by The Ecco Press in 1983
18 West 30th Street, New York, N.Y. 10001
Published simultaneously in Canada by
George J. McLeod, Ltd., Toronto
Printed in the United States of America
Library of Congress Catloging in Publication Data
Plumly, Stanley / Summer Celestial
(The American Poetry Series, Vol. 27)
I. Title.   II. Series
PS 3566.L78S9   1983   811'.54   83-5658
ISBN 0-88001-029-0

FIRST EDITION

Acknowledgments: *American Poetry Review:* "Ground Birds in Open
Country," "Virginia Beach"; *Antaeus:* "After Whistler," "Another
November," "Lapsed Meadow," "Nag's Head" (in another ver-
sion), "Wildflower"; *Antioch Review:* "Button Money"; *Atlantic
Monthly:* "Promising the Air"; *Crazy Horse:* "American Ash"; *Field:*
"Maples," "Two Moments, for My Mother"; *The Georgia Review:*
"Blossom," "Chertea," "Snowing, Sometimes"; *The Iowa Review:*
"After Rilke (1)"; *Memphis State Review:* "After Rilke (2)"; *The Mis-
souri Review:* "Sonnett"; *The New England Review:* "Waders and
Swimmers"; *The New Yorker:* "Commelina Virginica," "Fifth &
94th," "In Passing," "The Missionary Position," "Summer Celes-
tial," "Tree Ferns," "Valentine"; *The Ohio Review:* "Chinese Tal-
low"; *Ploughshares:* "Dark All Afternoon"; *Poetry:* "My Mother's
Feet," 'Posthumous Keats." The epigraph is from a verse letter to J.
H. Reynolds, March 25, 1818, Teignmouth. "Posthumous Keats"
was suggested by a paragraph from the chapter "Rome and the Last
Months" in the Walter Jackson Bate biography. The "After Rilke"
poems are versions of two in a sequence of poems entitled "The Book
of Poverty and Death." Many thanks to the National Endowment
for the Arts for a grant which helped start this book.

for Deborah Digges

Contents

❧ I ❧

Tree Ferns / 3

After Whistler / 4

Wildflower / 6

Valentine / 8

Chinese Tallow / 9

Ground Birds in Open Country / 10

In Passing / 12

Lapsed Meadow / 14

Posthumous Keats / 16

❧ II ❧

Promising the Air / 21

The Missionary Position / 22

Maples / 23

Chertea / 24

My Mother's Feet / 26

Two Moments, for My Mother / 27

Virginia Beach / 29

Sonnet / 31

Commelina Virginica / 32

Summer Celestial / 33

◂§ III §▸

Fifth & 94th / 37

Button Money / 38

Blossom / 39

After Rilke / 41

American Ash / 44

Waders and Swimmers / 46

Nag's Head / 48

Dark All Afternoon / 49

Snowing, Sometimes / 50

Another November / 52

I

Tree Ferns

They were the local Ohio palm, tropic in the heat of trains.
They could grow in anything—pitch, whole grain,
cinders, ash and rust, the dirt
dumped back of the foundry, what

the men wore home. Little willows,
they were made to be brushed back by the traffic of boxcars
the way wind will dust the shade
of the small part of a river. —They'd

go from almost green to almost gray with each long passing,
each leaf, each branch a stain
on the winded air. They were too thin
for rain—nothing could touch them.

So we'd start with pocketknives, cutting and whittling them
    down
from willow, palm, or any other name.
They were what they looked like. Horsewhip, whipweed.
They could lay on a fine welt if you wanted.

And on a hot, dry day, July, they could all but burn.
At a certain age you try to pull all kinds of things
out of the ground, out of the loose gravel thrown by trains.

Or break off what you can and cut it clean.

After Whistler

In his portrait of Carlyle, Whistler builds
from the color out: he calls it an arrangement
in gray and black and gives it a number in order
to commit us to the composition—to the foreground
first, in profile, before we go on to a wall
that seems to be neutral but is really the weather.
Carlyle is tired, beyond anger, and beautiful,
his white head tilted slightly toward the painter.
He is wearing a long coat and rests his hat on his knees.

When I was born I came out holding my breath, blue.
The cord had somehow rotted at the navel—
I must have lain alone for hours before they would let
my father's mother, the other woman there, give blood.
She still had red hair and four years to live.
The place on my arm where they put the needles in
I call my mortality scar. When I think of my grand-
mother lifting me all the way to the kitchen counter
I think of the weight by which we are doubled or more

through the lives of others. I followed her
everywhere, or tried to. I was her witness.
When I look at Whistler's portrait of Carlyle
I think of how the old survive: we make them up.
In the vegetable garden, therefore, the sun is gold
as qualified in pictures. She is kneeling in front
of the light in such a way I can separate skin from bone.
She is an outline, planting or preparing the ground.
For all I know she will never rise from this green place.

Even the painter's mother is staring into the future,
as if her son could paint her back into her body.
I was lucky. In nineteen thirty-nine they still
believed blood was family. In a room real
with walls the color of buckwheat she would sit out
the afternoon dressed up, rocking me to sleep.
It would be Sunday, slow, no one else at home.
And I would wake that way, small in her small arms,
hers, in the calendar dark, my head against her heart.

Wildflower

Some—the ones with fish names—grow so north
they last a month, six weeks at most.
Some others, named for the fields they look like,
last longer, smaller.

And these, in particular, whether trout or corn lily,
onion or bellwort, just cut
this morning and standing open in tapwater in the kitchen,
will close with the sun.

It is June, wildflowers on the table.
They are fresh an hour ago, like sliced lemons,
with the whole day ahead of them.
They could be common mayflower lilies of the valley,

day lilies, or the clustering Canada, large, gold,
long-stemmed as pasture roses, belled out over the vase—
or maybe Solomon's seal, the petals
ranged in small toy pairs

or starry, tipped at the head like weeds.
They could be anonymous as weeds.
They are, in fact, the several names of the same thing,
lilies of the field, butter-and-eggs,

toadflax almost, the way the whites and yellows juxtapose,
and have "the look of flowers that are looked at,"
rooted as they are in water, glass, and air.
I remember the summer I picked everything,

flower and wildflower, singled them out in jars
with a name attached. And when they had dried as stubborn
as paper I put them on pages and named them again.
They were all lilies, even the hyacinth,

even the great pale flower in the hand of the dead.
I picked it, kept it in the book for years
before I knew who she was,
her face lily-white, kissed and dry and cold.

Valentine

In summer they bunched like fruit, green
over green, lemon and lime,
darker on the sun side. Picked,
they looked like paper hearts—
pinned on paper, the way
we hung them up to dry at school.
They'd dry the color of the season.

This season I'm remembering climbing
onto the muscular branch of that
linden just to breathe, those nights
the second-story heat was bad enough
you had to sit it out. Moonlight
was cool coming down through the leaves—
it smelled of the earth dug at the root.

I let it cover me. I let it gather
on the ground into shadow
and small places, like water.
I'm remembering how clear things were
three or four in the morning twenty
feet above the day—I'm remembering
how I knew I had a soul because

it felt so good breathing this good air.
Luck is a tree branching to the roof
outside your window. I sat there, half asleep,
pulling off leaves, watching them disappear.
By dawn they were everywhere under me, gold,
silver, green, each the size of the hand
we lay on the sleep of children.

Chinese Tallow

I wanted to put the tree in the room,
the way the light in the morning
first fills, then surrounds it,
the way the light this morning brings it
to the window, brings it in, almost into the room.
And I wanted to bring the rain in with it,
the rain from all day yesterday, all night
until just now, the light filling the rain,
filled with the rain, the rain the light on the tree.

I did not want to wake in a room empty with air.
I did not want the shadow of the tree, blind sun.
I did not want the smell of it sweet in the room.
I did not want it brought in blessed with the thought of it.
I did not want it turned into something else,
branch and spider root, wet with possibilities.
I wanted to bring it in first light, shining, here.
I wanted it large with the rain inside it, filled with rain.
I wanted to wake in a room bright with small dark leaves.

Ground Birds in Open Country

They fly up in front of you,
suddenly, as in allegory, black
        and white, by the handful.
    If it's spring, they break
back and forth in a blur,
        in new air warm
        down to the ground. Lark
or longspur, starling or sparrow.

    My life list is one bird at a time long.
What Roethke calls *looking*.
        The eye, particular for color,
    remembers when a whole treeful
would go gray with applause.
        In the middle of nowhere,
        in a one-oak field.
I clapped my hands just for the company.

    As one lonely morning, green under glass,
a redwing flew straight at me,
        its shoulders slick with the air.
    It was that close,
and brilliant. In the birdbook, there,
    where the names are,
        it is always May,
and the thing so fixed we can see it,

    even the yellow margin halving the wing.
Magnolia, Blackpool, Palm and Pine—warblers:
        the time one got into the schoolroom
    we didn't know what it was,

but it sang, it sailed
along the ceiling on all sides.
And blew back out, wild, still lost,
before any of us, stunned, could shout it down.

And in a hallway once a bird went mad, window
by closed window, the hollow length of the building.
I had to break it, finally, with my hand.
They fly up so quickly
in front of you, without names,
in the slurred shapes of a wing.
Or they fly from room to room,
having already gathered in great numbers on the ground.

In Passing

On the Canadian side, we're standing far enough away
the Falls look like photography, the roar a radio.

In the real rain, so vertical it fuses with the air,
the boat below us is starting for the caves.

Everyone on deck is dressed in black, braced for weather
and crossing against the current of the river.

They seem lost in the gorge dimensions of the place,
then, in fog, in a moment, gone.

                              In the Chekhov story,
the lovers live in a cloud, above the sheer witness of a valley.

They call it circumstance. They look up at the open wing
of the sky, or they look down into the future.

Death is a power like any other pull of the earth.
The people in the raingear with the cameras want to see it

from the inside, from behind, from the dark looking into the
     light.
They want to take its picture, give it size—

how much easier to get lost in the gradations of a large
and yellow leaf drifting its good-bye down one side of the
     gorge.

There is almost nothing that does not signal loneliness,
then loveliness, then something connecting all we will become.

All around us the luminous passage of the air,
the flat, wet gold of the leaves. I will never love you

more than at this moment, here in October,
the new rain rising slowly from the river.

Lapsed Meadow

Wild has its skills.
The apple grew so close to the ground
it seemed the whole tree
    was thicket, crab and root—

    by fall it looked
like brush among burdock and hawkweed;
looked as if brush had been piled,
    for burning, at the center.

    At the edges, blurred,
like failed fence, the hawthorns, by
comparison, seemed planted.
    Everywhere else there was broom

    grass and timothy
and wood fern and sometimes a sapling,
sometimes a run of hazel. In Ohio,
    some people call it

    a farmer's field, all fireweed
and thistle, a waste of nature. And true,
you could lose yourself
    in the mind of the thing,

    especially summer, in the full
sun or later, after rain and the smell
of rain—you could lose
    yourself, waist- or head-high,

branch by leaf by branch.
There could be color, the kind that opens
and the kind that closes up,
one for each part

of the light; there might
be fruit, green or grounded—it was always
skin-tight, small and hard.
There would be goldenrod

still young or yellowing
in season, and wind enough to seed a countryside
of plows and pasture.
But I call it crazy

the way that apple,
in the middle of a field, dug in, part of the year
bare-knuckled, part of the year
blossoming.

for James Wright

\

Posthumous Keats

The road is so rough Severn is walking,
and every once in a while, since the season is
beautiful and there are flowers on both sides,
as if this path had just been plowed,
he picks by the handful what he can

and still keep up. Keats is in the carriage
swallowing blood and the best of the bad food.
It is early November, like summer,
honey and wheat in the last of the
daylight, and above the mountains a clear

carnelian heartline. Rome is a week
away. And Severn has started to fill
the carriage with wildflowers—rust, magenta,
marigold, and the china white of cups.
Keats is floating, his whole face luminous.

The biographer sees no glory in this,
how the living, by increments, are dead,
how they celebrate their passing half in love.
Keats, like his young companion, is alone,
among color and a long memory.

In his head he is writing a letter
about failure and money and the ten-
thousand lines that could not save his brother.
But he might as well be back at Gravesend
with the smell of the sea and cold sea rain,

waiting out the weather and the tide—
he might as well be lying in a room,
in Rome, staring at a ceiling stylized
with roses or watching outside right now
a cardinal with two footmen shooting birds.

He can still remember the meadows near
St. Cross, the taste in the air of apples,
the tower and alms-square, and the River
Itchen, all within the walk of a mile.
In the poem it is Sunday, the middle

of September, the light a gold conglomerate
of detail—"in the same way that some pictures
look warm." He has closed his eyes.
And he is going to let the day close down.
He is thinking he must learn Italian.

By the time they reach the Campagna the wind
will be blowing, the kind that begins at sea.
Severn will have climbed back in, finally a
passenger, with one more handful to add
to what is already overwhelming.

II

Promising the Air

A woman I loved talked in her sleep to children.
She would start her half of the conversation,
her half of asking, of answering the need to bring
the boy up the path from some dream-lake, some

wandering source, water, a river, or a road along
the tree-line of a river, she would say his small name,
then silence, privacy, the drift back to the center.
The child was the tenderness in her voice.

I can remember waking myself up talking, saying nothing
that mattered but loud enough for someone else to hear.
No one was there. It was like coming alive, suddenly,
in a body. I was afraid, as in the dark we are each time

new. I was afraid, word of mouth, out of breath.
Waking is the first loneliness—
but sleep can be anything you want, the path
to the summerhouse, silence, or a call across water.

I am taught, and believe, that even in light the mind
wanders, speaks before thinking. This piece of a poem
is for her who wept without waking, who, word for word,
kept her promise to the air. And for the boy.

The Missionary Position

Even the light coming down is slick with rain.
And the wind with its small cups filled.
I have opened my eyes in the dark in a dream
of people trying to pass from one high place
to the next. Each roof slopes sharp with tiles.
I cannot catch them, no one. They slip from me
like parts of myself, like parts of another body.
If I watch, face within face, if I look down,
as at a wound, I know I will not wake whole.

                                    As it is
I have opened my eyes in the dark, without parents,
unable to open my hands. But I can hear the oak
outside make its own green passage, I can see light
just under the window, under the shadow of glass
on the wall. This is not what I wanted. I was
in love. I was one blind body moving over another.
I am going to lie here until I fall back to sleep.
I am going to close my eyes and think my way back.
I am going to let the rain come down, all over me.

Maples

In a wheat field, at evening, the wheat
still green, and torn, a blown red maple
eighty, ninety feet to the crown. . . .

The wind, you said, seemed to have crossed
all of Canada to get here, had hit the tree hard.
Leaves, limbs, almost a whole half gone.

I was in your arms, asleep. We had stopped,
as we had stopped before between small Ontario towns.
You would quarrel about distances,

the setting of the sun. Brampton, Port Elgin.
You were in love, big sky, a few big stars.
And always, in cold country, the dark coming on.

You told me we were lost a week,
my father so tanked up he dreamed at the wheel.
Some nights we spent the night in the car.

The moon you called your honeymoon,
something pure but piecemeal, as that night it sat
webbed in the high netting of half a tree.

What the wind, you said, had put there.

Chertea

You know its voice,
how it turns the air
through the needle's eye,
again and again and again,
a word that will not be

pronounced. You know
the tree—sycamore, December,
the birch bark clean,
the light what the snow
let in.

I cannot believe
a bird this morning,
the small, precise
discipline of the sound—
I cannot believe

one dead leaf alive,
the wind all night
blowing and calming
with the cold.
The tree is in the room,

a wound on the air.
My sister brought birds home
furred with ice.
She carried them
as if to heal them.

She knew what she knew
she had heard—teacher, teacher,
story, story, story.
The dream out loud
will not say as much,

nor waking out of season.
In the Dickinson gray and granular
white of the past
the light coming in
is clear,

so that
when she held them up
to the window, both hands,
the color seemed to bleed
back into them.

My Mother's Feet

How no shoe fit them,
and how she used to prop them,
having dressed for bed,
letting the fire in the coal-stove blue

and blink out, falling asleep in her chair.
How she bathed and dried them, night after night,
and rubbed their soreness like an intimacy.
How she let the fire pull her soft body through them.

She was the girl who grew just standing,
the one the picture cut at the knees.
She was the girl who seemed to be dancing
out on the lawn, after supper, alone.

I have watched her climb the militant stairs
and down again, watched the ground go out from under her.
I have seen her on the edge of chances—
she fell, when she fell, like a girl.

Someone who loved her said she walked on water.
Where there is no path nor wake. As a child
I would rise in the half-dark of the house,
from a bad dream or a noisy window,

something, almost, like snow in the air,
and wander until I could find those feet, propped
and warm as a bricklayer's hands,
every step of the way shining out of them.

Two Moments, for My Mother

(1)

Lacrimal, clavicle, patella—
bones of the body; clusters, corollas, pinwheels—

enough to make a metaphor of meadows. These are the signs
in the sky, these heavens in which a man will, forever,

carry water, and fish will fly.

                     Only a child would bother
to draw lines, to piece the dark together, to gather
fireflies—as in a field tonight, black from the body down,
I watched hundreds fill the air without pattern.

At a distance they would have made more sense.
But here they were beautiful, they were what they were.

I try to imagine what it will be like without you,
your body white as a candle. I cannot connect your death.

Gall-of-the-earth, snow-on-the-mountain,
what lasts is bone, or a small fire in the memory.

(2)

The nights I don't sleep, like the days I sleepwalk through—

I am thinking about your hand on my forehead,
how it let the pain shine, go dark, and cool,

how you sat there, hours, talking, saying my name,
telling the story of the new moon.

What you called a coal-star, red ash soft in the wind,
still blows down on the lawn. A sign, you said.

And who can sleep whose bed is not by the window?
The sky in the maple still turns and turns and lets the wind

in first, then rain, then a light that is nothing
but silver off the leaves.

                          I am alive because of you.
I am alive all night, and in the morning,
like a penny's worth of fever, the sun is alive,

one color, then another—lily, chrysanthemum, dew.

Virginia Beach

Those mornings in green mountains
when the air burned off blue,
        mornings of fog coming up
    from all night in the ground,
mornings when the sky was down again—

    one blind morning I stood numb
as a child knee-deep in saltwater
            waiting for the cloud to lift.
    It lifted. It rose
by disappearing, rain back into sunlight.

    Water is one thing on water,
another, like smoke, on a mountainside.
            Mornings I can imagine the men
    still go out along the Blue Ridge
to handcut trees—summer and winter,

    hickory and oak, sycamore and maple.
Nineteen forty-something-or-other.
        I still see my father
    sawing on my sister with a whip.
Virginia green. Sometimes when you love someone

    you think of pain—how to forgive
what is almost past memory.
        All you can remember is the name,
    some place you have in mind
where all the blue smoke, all the ghost water collects,

where the ground lets go. One year,
along the Shenandoah, the county flooded a farm.
        You could row out over the trees,
    the outbuildings, the barn, green.
You could almost see them down there drifting whole.

    The first time people see the ocean
they say they are afraid because they feel anonymous.
        What you need to name you save
        by saying it out loud.
You stand in the visible, blue air, sure that your voice

will carry, clear that it will all come back in another form.

Sonnet

Whatever it is, however it comes, it takes time.
It can take all night.
My father would sit on the edge of the bed
and let the tears fall to the floor,
the sun the size of the window, full
and rising. He was a dead man and he knew it.

I think of him almost every time I fall in love,
how the heart is three-quarters high in the body.
—He could lift his own weight above his head.
—He could run a furrow straight by hand.
I think of him large in his dark house,
hard in thought, taking his time.

But in fact he is sitting on the edge of the bed,
and it is morning, my mother's arms around him.

Commelina Virginica

Sky-high the light would be gold already,
the morning having come down part and piecemeal—
gentian, violet, forget-me-not, a ladder's
length of blue. Breakfast and bitching and the first
big trees swallowing, it seemed, the sound of everything—
I was so close to the ground all I could
hear was falling. That was nineteen forty-
three, almost the first year I remember.
I loved rising early among these men
my father loved—coffee and biscuits,
bacon on the grill,
the smoke from the fire the same as the air—
I loved the way the air took color from the leaves.
The dayflowers I picked because they were blue
and delicate, almost, as ash drifting,
and had two petals larger than the third
and disappeared in hand and left no stain.
I picked them again and again, and let

them go, or thought I did. The whole day ahead
the smell of fresh-cut wood and putting things in my pockets—

Summer Celestial

At dusk I row out to what looks like light or anonymity,
too far from land to be called to, too close to be lost,
and drag oar until I can drift in and out of a circle,
the center of a circle, nothing named, nothing now to see,
the wind up a little and down, building against the air,
and listen to anything at all, bird or wind, or nothing
but the first sounds on the surface, clarifying, clear.

Once, in Canada, I saw a man stand up in his boat and pass
out dollar bills. It was summer dark. They blew down
on the lake like moonlight. Coming out of his hands
they looked like dollar bills. When I look up at the Dippers,
the whole star chart, leaves on a tree, sometimes all night,
I think about his balance over cold water, under stars,
standing in a shoe, the nets all down and gathering.

My mother still wakes crying do I think she's made of money.
—And what makes money make money make money?
I wish I could tell her how to talk herself to sleep.
I wish. She says she's afraid she won't make it back.
As in a prayer, she is more afraid of loneliness than death.
Two pennies for the eyes, two cents: I wish I could tell her
that each day the stars reorganize, each night they come back
  new.

Outside tonight the waters run to color with the sky.
In the old water dream you wake up in a boat, drifting out.
Everything is cold and smells of rain. Somewhere back there,
in sleep, you remember weeping. And at this moment you
  think
you are about to speak. But someone is holding on, hand
over hand, and someone with your voice opening and closing.
In water you think it will always be your face that floats

to the surface. Flesh is on fire under water. The nets go back
to gather and regather, and bring up stones, viridian and silver,
what falls. In the story, the three Dutch fishermen sail out
for stars, into the daylight hours, so loaded with their catch
it spills. They sleep, believe it, where they can, and dry
their nets on a full moon. For my mother, who is afraid to
      sleep,
for anyone afraid of heights or water, all of this is intolerable.

Look, said the wish, into your lover's face. Mine over yours.
In that other life, which I now commend to you, I have spent
the days by a house along the shore, building a boat, tying
the nets together, watching the lights go on and off on the
      water.
But nothing gets done, none of it ever gets finished. So I lie
      down
in a dream of money being passed from hand to hand in a long
      line.
It looks like money—or hands taking hands, being led out

to deeper water. I wake up weeping, and it is almost joy.
I go outside and the sky is sea-blue, the way the earth is looked
      at
from the moon. And out on the great surfaces, water is paying
back water. I know, I know this is a day and the stars reiterate,
return each loss, each witness. And that always in the room
      next door
someone is coughing all night or a man and a woman make
      love,
each body buoyed, even blessed, by what the other cannot
      have.

III

Fifth & 94th

People are standing, as if out of the rain,
holding on. For the last two blocks
the woman across the aisle has wept
quietly into her hands, the whole
of her upper body nodding, keeping time.
The bus is slow enough you can hear,
inside your head, the traffic within
traffic, like another talk.

Someone is leaning down, someone has touched
her shoulder. But by now she has tucked
her legs up under her, grief given over.
She will not lift her face.
Across the park the winter sun is perfect
behind the grill-work of the trees,
as here it is brilliant against buildings.
Above her body the thousand windows blur.

Button Money

You might as well pray for rain.
In any other form it came in snow
or the aluminum color of the fog.
Or in clear blocks from the back
of the truck, hooked on two sides,
shouldered into the house like
buckets of water. That summer
salt and flour and meat still tasted
like paper, butter never quite yellow.
The war was four years old, poor,
a stone tossed at a train.
You paid for it in small red coin,
in windows bright with the gold
and silver medals of the dead.
Nothing to buy, nothing to spend—
I had my pockets full, burrowing
through the shade on the brickwalk,
head down, hard on my bike for
the iceman. It was always evening,
the radios on on the porches,
the parents at watch as if the day
might end without them. At the corner
you could chip the ice off clean
for a penny, all you could hold.

Blossom

And after a while he'd say his head was a rose,
a big beautiful rose, and he was going to blow it
all over the room, he was going to blast blood.

And after a while he'd just put his head in his one good
hand the way children do who want to go into hiding.

I still can't get the smell of smoke from a woodstove out of my
    head.
A woman is frying bacon and the odor is char and sour and
    somebody
running a finger over your tongue. All those dead years and the
    grease

still glue on the wall. In Winchester, Virginia, the year the war
ended, the blacks were still dark clouds. My uncle had a knife
pulled on him holding his nose.

                              When the Guard marched
        eleven
German prisoners of war down from Washington they
    marched them
right through town, and it was spring and a parade like apple
    blossom.
Black and white, we lined up just to watch.

I still can't get the smell of apples out of my head—
trees in orchards all over the county, like flowers in a garden.
The trees the Germans planted that spring looked like flowers,

thin as whips. Even so the branch of a full-grown apple tree
is tested every summer: when I didn't watch I picked along
        with
every black boy big enough to lift a bushel. Frederick County.

The National Guard in nineteen forty-five was my father and
        any
other son who stayed home. Next door the father of my friend
had been home two long years, one arm, one leg gone. He was

honorary. He was white sometimes, and black, depending.
He was leaf and woodsmoke and leaning always into the wind.

And everybody called him Blossom because of the piece of
        apple
he kept tucked at one side of his mouth. When he was drinking
he'd bring his bottle over and talk to my father about Germans.

They go down, he'd say, they all go down on their guns.

Each five-petaled flower on the tree means an apple come
        summer.
I still can't get the bourbon smell of Blossom out of my head.
He spits his apple out and shoots himself in the mouth with his
        finger.

After Rilke

(1)

There is the poverty of children shy with child—
the girl who will not say what is already
part of her breath, like a second wind, another mouth.
And there is the poverty of rain, in spring,
clean on the streets, the small roofs of the city.
And poverty of desire in prison hallways, cell by cell. . . .

And poverty of the wheelchair and the deathbed
and the blind who tow them where they're told.
Or flowers along the railway and the river,
poorer with every passage.

           You should look
into your hands right now—they'll hold
the poverty of grief until you let it go.

You should look into the light—it is the dust made whole.

The poverty of the bird that flies in the window
or the yard-dog tied to the ground—rooms with doors
locked on the dumb who talk to themselves. . . .
These are the stones that will shine.

For the poor own the houses you will not visit;
they own the trees that are dead all day.
They own the table and the chair and the glass of water.

And they let their children go hungry who will eat all the
    bread.

And they let their children go cold who will take what is
    warm.

You should look around you how the dark is poor.

(2)

And, Masters, how all this city planning comes
to one dead-end or another—block after block
abandoned, as in the loneliness after a fire.
This could be snow falling through the roof, nineteen
hundred and one, or the air that will open above Dresden.

I have seen people stunned, sitting in the center of their rooms,
watching the street like children who have sinned.
I have seen a child's shadow, the shadow of a child,
at the same sill the same each day.
And nowhere in the mind of that child

nor in what its father sees
is the shade tree rooted where the ground is green
or the wind off water and the sea rose bending.
The sad eyes looking back at me
give nothing for nothing.

And the girls, so young they still bloom toward the future
and seem almost beautiful with memory,
though we know what they long for is beyond desire,
their bodies burning even as they close,
they will be mothers, year after year,

and will sit at tables half in, half out of light,
waiting for something as at the hour assigned
in a room adjacent where they can be alone
and be at peace and let themselves lie down in a long death,
still married to need and the needs of others.

American Ash

The day is late enough you could stand
within the time it takes a door to drift
back shut and watch half a tree go dark,
the other half still green with the afternoon.
I have in mind the big one down the street,
west of the house, the light so stacked and split
it bottles up, brilliant at the top.
Downing going the other way is shade.
Upstairs the light is candle-in-a-shell.
Someone is getting ready to go to bed.
The house is rich with camphor, mint, and oil
of wintergreen, and on the dining table
roses in a bowl.
               I think it is nineteen
forty-five. Sepia will never get
quite right the year in color, my mother's
dress, for instance, red and yellow daisies
on a regimental blue to end the war,
nor my father home from work to work his garden.
He has a lantern. It is almost May,
the streetlights coming on, one to a corner.
If it is true the soul is other people,
then the antique finish of the thing
is how we love the past, how the aging
of a photograph becomes, like leaves, deciduous.
At the head of the stairs my mother's
mother's bedroom and beside hers the mahogany
and cedar of her father's . . . For a hundred years
the sun has set against the high side of the house.
I could climb those stairs, I could sleep and be
filled with the dead odors of moths and wools

and silks, with the sweet addictions of the flesh.
I could float a little lifetime above the kitchen talk,
branch, green, the sudden burden of the leaves.

Waders and Swimmers

The first morning it flew out of the fog
I thought it lived there.
It floated into shore all shoulders,
all water and air. It was cold that summer.
In the white dark the sun coming up was the moon.
And then this beautiful bird,
its wings as large as a man, drawing the line
of itself out of the light behind it.
A month or more it flew out of the fog,
fished, fed, gone in a moment.

There are no blue herons in Ohio.
But one October in a park I saw a swan
lift itself from the water in singular, vertical strokes.
It got high enough to come back down wild.
It ate bread from the hand
and swallowed in long, irregular gestures.
It seemed, to a child, almost angry.
I remember what I hated
when someone tied it wing-wide to a tree.
The note nailed to its neck said this is nothing.

The air is nothing, though it rise
and fall. Another year
a bird the size of a whooping crane
flew up the Hocking—
people had never seen a bird that close
so large and white at once.
They called it their ghost and went back to their Bibles.
It stood on houses for days, lost,

smoke from the river.
In the wing-light of the dawn it must have passed

its shadow coming and going. I wish I knew.
I still worry a swan alive
through an early Ohio winter, still worry
its stuttering, clipped wings.
It rises in snow, white on white, the way
in memory one thing is confused with another.
From here to a bird that flies
with its neck folded back to its shoulders
is nothing but air, nothing but first light and summer
and water rising in a smoke of waters.

Merriman's Cove, Maine

Nag's Head

The weather starts at sea-level—ten-, twelve-,
twenty-story clouds. Down the beach the old men
let their kites lift in wind big enough
to blow them over. Even the shorebirds

hover, move in place. It is almost noon,
July. I wish I could say the sun rose out
of the water this morning leaf by gold
leaf. It came up salt and sour with the air.

Now the women are wading in it white.
In winter sometimes, by the pictures, the tides
wash all the way to the third floors, high as
the hotels. They still start at the horizon,

though for a long mile or so you can watch
the water shipwreck, plow under, work its
way on in on the backs of the swimmers.
By three, the water will be stone—

it will break a hundred times by the handful
in this light. Wind will make it look like
snow piling at the beach its ocean ice.
It is already the stony color of a shell.

The locals used to live by lighting fires
for boats lost in the shallows just off shore.
The story is that only property was saved,
the bodies stacked like timber to be burned.

Dark All Afternoon

The boats are rented, complete with open sail,
as if there were a map, somewhere to go,
somewhere besides the cold and nautical
Charles, one river wide, up and down, and slow.
Even the moon right now, in love, in cloud,
is set, half full, something to be filled,
something about the sun the water healed.

We will not die in our sleep in Boston.
But there are days by a river the light
begins to end from the morning on,
and the boats, insomniac, adrift, will not
come in. The leaves are gold or gone, the sky
blue beautiful with cloud, snow in the air
or rain. But the boats, inevitably,

will not come in.

for Laura Jensen

Snowing, Sometimes

You couldn't keep it out.
You could see it drifting
from one side of the road
to the other—you could watch
the wind work it back and forth
across the hard white surfaces.
You could see the maple, with
its ten dead leaves, winded,
wanting it. But sometimes
you couldn't keep it out.

It was like dust, an elegance,
like frost. All you had to
do was stand at the window
and it passed, like the light,
over your face—softer than light
at the edges, the seams,
the separations in the glass.
All you had to do was stand
still in the dark and the room
seemed alive with it, crystalline,
a bright breath on the air.

If you fell asleep you knew
it could cover you, cover you
the way cold closes on water.
It would shine, like ice,
inside you. If you woke up
early, the cup on the bureau
cracked, you were sure that

even the pockets of your pants,
hung on the back of the chair,
would be filled. Nothing could
stop it, could keep it out.

Not the room in sunlight, nor
smoky with the rain. Not
the mother sweeping, nor
building the woodfire each
morning. Not the wind blowing
backwards, without sound.
Not the boy at the window
who loves the look of it
dusting the ground, whiter
than flour, piled in the

small, far corners.

Another November

In the blue eye of the medievalist there is a cart in the road.
There are brushfires and hedgerows and smoke and smoke
and the sun gold dollop going down.

The light has been falling all afternoon and the rain off and on.
There is a picture of a painting in a book in which the surface
of the paper, like the membrane of the canvas,

is nothing if not a light falling from another source.
The harvest is finished and figure, ground, trees lined up
      against
the sky all look like furniture—

even the man pushing the cart that looks like a chair,
even the people propped up in the fields, gleaning, or watching
the man, waving his passage on.

Part of a cloud has washed in to clarify or confound.
It is that time of the day between work and supper when the
      body
would lie down, like bread, or is so much of a piece

with the whole it is wood for a fire. Witness how
it is as difficult to paint rain as it is this light falling across
this page right now because there will always be

a plague of the luminous dead being wheeled to the edge of
      town.
The painting in the book is a landscape in a room, cart in the
      road,
someone's face at the window.

A Note About the Author

*Stanley Plumly was born in Barnesville, Ohio, and grew up
in the lumber and farming regions of Virginia and Ohio.
He has taught at several universities, most recently at Columbia,
and the Universities of Washington, Houston, and Iowa.
His* In the Outer Dark *won the Delmore Schwartz Memorial Award,
and* Out-of-the-Body Travel *was nominated for a National Book
Critics Circle Award in 1978. He has held a Guggenheim Fellowship
and has been the recipient of a National
Endowment for the Arts Fellowship.*